Transformation

A collection of poems to
heal and replenish the spirit

SUE TREDGET

CAUSEWAY PUBLISHING

Published in Western Australia by
Causeway Publishing
Wembley Downs, WA 6019
Phone: 0422 228 502
Web: www.suetredget.com

First published in Australia 2017
Copyright © Sue Tredget 2017

All rights reserved. No part of this publication may be
reproduced, stored in a retrieval system, or transmitted,
in any form or by any means without the prior written
permission of the publisher, nor be otherwise circulated
in any form of binding or cover other than that in which
it is published and without a similar condition being
imposed on the subsequent purchaser.

 A catalogue record for this book is available from the National Library of Australia

Creator: Sue Tredget
Title: Transformation
ISBN: 978-0-9876171-5-6 (Paperback)
ISBN: 978-0-6480901-3-7 (ebook)

Cover design and layout: Rhianna King Creative
(www.rhiannaking.com.au)

Disclaimer
All care has been taken in the preparation of the
information herein, but no responsibility can be accepted
by the publisher or author for any damages resulting from
the misinterpretation of this work. All contact details
given in this book were current at the time of publication,
but are subject to change.

For Julie Baker

Contents

Travelling light	1
Clarity	5
A different hue	6
What lies beyond	7
I rise above	8
Contrasts	9
Mother Nature	10
The tear	12
A beginning	13
Down by the lake	14
Expansion	15
Bench	16
Damaged	17
Should and shouldn't	18
Disappointment	19
Camino	20
Possibility	21
Coffee catch up	22
Spring clean	25
Reaching out	26
Light and shade	28
Inspired (by Chelsea)	29
A new song	30
80s mash up	31
Black Dog	33
A fairy tale ending	36
Acknowledgements	38

*Poetry is the spontaneous overflow of
powerful feelings:
it takes its origin from emotion recollected
in tranquility.*
~William Wordsworth, Lyrical Ballads

Preface

TRAVELLING LIGHT

A few years ago I was carrying around at least five oversized suitcases of baggage. It came with me everywhere, although plane travel was clearly out of the question. No airport trolley could accommodate my five suitcases and my excess baggage costs would have far exceeded even the most expensive of fares. One day I became so overwhelmed by how cumbersome and heavy it all was that I simply collapsed under the strain the weight was putting on my mind and body. It became so difficult to haul it all around with me that I just gave up trying and refused to move for a while. Well actually for quite a long time.

I eventually realised that in order to move from my solitary spot I was going to have to start shedding some of the baggage that was encircling me. Gradually I chipped away at it and after many months I found myself with just one, albeit still quite large suitcase. I stood up, and began to move, slowly at first, and then more purposefully, and my suitcase glided along behind me quite comfortably on its four wheels. One day when I was engrossed in a project I had started working on I looked behind me and was astonished to find that my oversized luggage had shrunk to a neat carry-on sized case. I'd felt the lightening of the load but was still startled at how much my burden had lessened. I was overjoyed.

These days I tend to carry around a nice light-weight day pack or a practical over the shoulder messenger bag, occasionally an attractive sparkly clutch, and now and again I can fit all my baggage into one very small bum bag. It's so great to travel light. I cannot recommend it highly enough.

It was writing more than anything else that allowed me to lighten my load. In *Changing Lightbulbs* I document my journey through, and recovery from, depression and anxiety. In this little companion book I offer you some words in verse, words that helped me to heal and replenish my spirit along the way. I hope you like them, and I hope they will encourage you to find your creative voice and express yourself in the way that suits you best.

Clarity

Embrace possibility
Banish the doubt
Reject negativity
Let your words out
In the space between moments
All becomes clear
No more anxiety
A life beyond fear.

A different hue

My name is Sue
I once was blue
But listen as I say to you
My life now has a different hue.

The indigo of midnight skies
The patterned wings of butterflies
The orange glow of rising sun
Red fiery skies when day is done
The softest white of falling snow
Bright fields of tulips row on row
The golden tones of daffodils
The evening light on distant hills
The earthy tones of autumn leaves
The green of all the plants and trees
Or any mix of all of these.

TRANSFORMATION

Sometimes the blue creeps in again
But that's OK, it always ends
For now I know just what to do
To add more colour to my blue.

What lies beyond

Beyond the confines of the mind there lies a place
Where thoughts are pure as morning dew
On an early winter's day when air is crisp
and sky the clearest blue.
Outside the prison of doubt and fear there is a space
Where words flow clearly like a mountain stream
Filled with melting snows of spring,
so fresh and pure and clean.
All is still and calm and quiet and soft and warm
In this sacred place where I yearn to linger
And bask in clarity of thought and word and deed
And bathe in the blessed light of peace and love.

Contrasts

The calm we feel before the storm
The long dark night before the dawn
The pain that comes before relief
The anger that is part of grief
Forgiveness comes if we accept
Belonging if we just connect
With the wonder all around
If we seek it will be found
The answer lies within us all
We pick ourselves up when we fall
We take the time to heal and mend
And know that all things have to end
We find the truth inside and out
And banish anguish, fear and doubt.

Mother Nature

You warm me up when I am cold
You hold my hand as I grow old
When I fragment you make me whole
When I'm bereft you soothe my soul
You're with me in the black of night
You bathe me in your healing light
When I am lost you show the way
You're with me as dark turns to day
When I am weak you make me strong
You make it right when all seems wrong
When I am low you lift me high
You gently wipe the tears I cry
When I am small you help me grow
You tell me why when I don't know
You hold me in your warm embrace
Your soothing rays soft on my face
You cradle me in loving arms
You heal me with your endless charms
You always change, yet stay the same
Help me forgive instead of blame

TRANSFORMATION

You guide me when I come apart
I hear your pulse within my heart
You're always there, will never leave
You hear my pain, you help me grieve
You share my joy and ease my strife
You are the constant in my life.

The tear

You turned your back and walked away
You did not let me have my say
You shut me down, you closed me out
You made it clear, I had no doubt
That you no longer were my friend
The tear too great to ever mend.

A beginning

I have a sense of a beginning now
Something has ended, run its course
It's time to step away
from what is old and worn and tired
And take a leap into the void
To find what's new, embrace what lies ahead
What lies above and all around
In stillness, calm, and silence, it will be found.

Down by the lake

Down by the lake I dream of all things good and true
Of gentle days and sacred ways, of places old and new
Of gardens tended through the years
to hold us in their spell.

Down by the lake I watch the fading light at end of day
The purple pink of wispy clouds
The swirling trails and misty shrouds
Reflected in the rippling mirror
as I stand by water's edge.

Bench

What stories you could tell
of those who sat in contemplation
The sights and sounds of nature
bringing solace to their desolation
As they grieved their losses,
calmed their thoughts, wept silent tears
For sadness and betrayal, for the hurt across the years.
And all the while the water shines
and shimmers under quiet autumnal sun
As peace creeps into troubled minds,
the healing now begun.

Expansion

To contract or to expand, I wondered what to do
It took some time before I knew
I shrivelled up before I grew
I cowered in silence in the gloom
In the empty corner of the room
With no way out, or so it seemed.

Until a different kind of day arrived
So unexpected, not contrived
The day on which I came alive
The endless months of dark descending
Would finally have a happy ending
A day like any other day, or so I thought.

Until a glimpse of sky between the clouds of May
Allowed the sun to show the way
And there you were, and then I knew
I knew just what I had to do
I stepped into the open space
I sang my song, I found my place.

I rise above

I rise above your poisoned heart
Your sad corrupted core
Your cowardly deeds and empty words
Your lies and your deceit
Your thoughtless acts and scheming ways
That leave all in their wake
To tip toe through the shards of hurt and loss
That you create, no mercy shown.
Your thirst for power, your endless quest
To control and to divide
Will never drag me down.
Your puerile mind games
Will not break my strength.
I retain the essence of myself
My calm, my truth, my light
I rise above, I glow, I shine
I walk away, my spirit filled with hope
And my heart replete with love
I rise above.

Damaged

We are all damaged goods
Repaired by the warp and weft of tiny threads
Held together with sticky tape and glue.
Sometimes the joins cannot be seen
The scars a tiny silvery line
On otherwise unblemished skin.
But now and then they reappear
The crazy paving of our cracks seems more defined
Our scars reflect our state of mind
They raise and turn an angry red
When doubts descend.
Until we breathe more clearly once again
And calm returns as we expel infection
And gaze again with calm accepting love
At our reflection.

Should and shouldn't

You should feel this, should not feel that
You should be more like me,
Just shut it out and close it down
You shouldn't cry and fret and frown.

But I am me, and only me
Please allow me just to be
Please don't deny my right to feel
The ebb and flow, the wax and wane
Just give me time to start again
These feelings aren't made up, they're real
Just give me time and I will heal.

Disappointment

I cannot bear again to see the resignation in your eyes
The disappointment on your face
The way you look at me with weary sighs.

I cannot bear to hear your disapproving judgement
Of what you do not understand
Your impatient words as I retreat again
Into the blackening night
Why can't you just reach out your hand?

I cannot bear it any more
I want to sleep for evermore.

Camino

A new day dawns, bringing inspiration
Can I make it happen, this transformation?
Stopped in a church along the way
Sat in the sacred silence to pray.
Gentle Hans with his arm in a sling
Spoke of his life, made my soul sing.
Stopped by a stream, fresh and cool
Weary feet bathed in a sacred pool.
Walked with my friend, spoke for a while
Our hearts united, she makes me smile.
My muscles are aching, my ligaments torn
But my spirit soars, I am reborn.

Possibility

Today is a day when all seems possible
When doors are open wide instead of half closed
When cups overflow and sustenance abounds
When all we see is beauty, and all we hear is joyful sounds.

A day to laugh and dance and sing
And count our many blessings
And give thanks to the mysteries we'll never comprehend
Which fill our spirits with hope and love
With purest thoughts and gratitude
For all that's been, and all that's yet to come.

Coffee catch up

I'd love to meet for coffee
I'd love to have a chat
But I'll have my phone in front of me
Oh sorry, what was that?
I'll put it on the table as I wouldn't want to miss
What someone else is sending out
With a smiley face and kiss
So tell me what's been going on
I know you've had it tough
I heard that you'd been feeling low
Been through some dreadful stuff
Now just lean in beside me
You can make a funny face
I'll send this out to all my friends
And I must just tag this place
So they know what fun we're having
Now what was that you said?
Oh look, three friends just liked my post
What's that, is someone dead?

And did you say you'd left your job?
Oh come on now, don't cry
Hey look at this, it's really fun
Gosh, did she really die?
I know it's very sad and all
But she wasn't a close friend
Oh look at who's just come online
An awful way to end
It's time that you felt better now
And move on, like I say
I won't get that, it's just my boss
I called in sick today
Oh look at who's just come online
I must just check his post
I can't eat that I'm gluten free
You know I don't eat toast
Another message just popped up
I really need to check
Oh shit he says he's going to leave
I might just break his neck
I'm sorry but I'll have to go
And try and sort this out
We had an argument last night

TRANSFORMATION

He's starting to have doubts
We must meet up again next week
I really have to run
Just text me with a time and place
It's been a lot of fun.

Spring clean

(with apologies to W H Auden)

Clear out the pantry, shake off the dust
Polish the silver and scrape off the rust
Throw away what you don't need, take clutter to the tip
Empty out the dustbin, put rubbish in the skip
Throw the heavy curtains wide and let the sunlight in
Open all the windows, and let the day begin.

Reaching out

Brother sister Mum and Dad
You were so far away
Did I not hear when you called out
Did I not listen to your shout?

Across the world, ten thousand miles
Did you need me there?
To hold your hand in darkest night
To heal the wounds and make it right?

Did you not hear me scream and sob
Or feel my blank despair?
Did you not hear me gnash my teeth?
Black dogs have no respect for grief.

Brother sister, why did death
Snatch them all away?
Our big sister, Mum and Dad
The pain too deep, the saddest sad.

We all grieve in different ways
But in the midst of loss
We struggled to communicate
I really hope it's not too late

For us to heal the wounds we made
With our thoughtless words
The silent anger broke my heart
The gaping hole tore me apart.

We need to stand upon the bridge
Let troubled waters flow
We need to speak with kind respect
With opens hearts, to reconnect.

I hope we will do that one day
I really don't know when
Perhaps this year, perhaps we can,
Or maybe next, let's make a plan.

Inspired (by Chelsea)

Inspired tonight, inspired by you
Inspired to be, inspired to do
Inspired to dream, inspired to feel
Inspired to always keep it real
Inspired to sing, inspired to dance
Inspired to dare, to take a chance.

When life dealt you the cruelest blow
You chose to live, you chose to grow
You chose to love instead of fear
Your will was strong, your mind was clear
You chose to stay true to your path
You chose to play, you chose to laugh
You chose to learn from tragedy
Create your own new destiny.

Inspired tonight, inspired by you
Inspired to be, inspired to do.

Light and shade

Light and shade
Day and night
Blackest blackest
And whitest white.

Stormy seas
Waters wild
Dying man
New born child.

Scorching sun
Pouring rain
Cooling breeze
Ease the pain.

Summer winter
Drifting snow
Autumn Spring
Moonlight glow.

TRANSFORMATION

Rest and play
Sleep and wake
Raging torrent
Peaceful lake.

Roaring lion
Gentle dove
Light and shade
Hate and love.

There is no dawn
Without the night
And dark will always
Lead to light.

A new song

I'm dancing to a different beat
I'm singing a new song
I'm walking tall and standing straight
I've found the right, beyond the wrong.

I'm talking a new language now
I'm playing a new game
I'm jumping high up in the air
I've found the joy beyond the pain.

I'm dancing with a new tribe now
I'm running a new race
I'm learning how to soar above
I've found my home, my sacred space.

80s mash up

With apologies to all the artists who wrote the soundtrack of my youth and whose lyrics I have shamelessly plagiarised

I'm sending out an SOS
For I'm the king of pain
Love doesn't live here anymore
I'm drowning in the purple rain.

But now I'm hungry like the wolf
And I was born to run
I saw the whole of the full moon
I'm welcome in the house of fun.

I feel just like a virgin
I've found my lucky star
I'm going on a holiday
I'm dancing in the dark.

Wake me up before you go
Don't want to miss a thing
My love's not tainted anymore
I fixed this broken wing.

I'm never going to give you up
I'll keep on loving you
I'm here with every breath you take
I know this much is true.

I'm finally learning how to fly
I'm living on a prayer
There's something in the air tonight
Just hold my hand, I'll take you there.

Black Dog

I had a black dog for a while
He came to stay one day
He'd kept a watch outside my house
Waiting for a chance to pounce.

I think he'd had me in his sights
For a year or two
He licked his lips and circled round
As I sank slowly underground.

I didn't know that he was there
I didn't understand
His sharp teeth sank into my arm
And blood dripped slowly down my hand.

He stayed beside me day and night
He wouldn't let me go
He watched my life force drain away
I thought that he was here to stay.

I said that I was quite alright
And noone really knew
But I was just an empty shell
He made my mind a silent hell.

He fixed me with his glassy stare
And breathed his rancid breath
Each night he curled up by my bed
While twisted thoughts swirled in my head.

For months he stayed right by my side
Came with me everywhere
From bed to couch and back again
I couldn't fight, I didn't care.

Then something changed in early Spring
And he began to stray
I heard a distant call one night
And step by step he moved away.

I found a leash and tamed the beast
And slowly I grew strong
I learnt to keep him at arms length
And found a new way to belong.

TRANSFORMATION

I let the lead out bit by bit
Each day I grew more brave
And as he moved away from me
I saw the person I could be.

Then every day I let him run
Across the fields of green
'Til one fine day I looked around
And he was nowhere to be seen.

I know he's skulking in the woods
I feel his clammy breath
But I won't let him pounce again
He won't come back to claim my death.

If my black dog finds you one day
Don't ever give up hope
Don't let him win, don't ever think
That you can't come back from the brink.

The black dog is no friend of mine
But in a way I see
I needed him to help me grow
He led me to a brand new me.

A fairy tale ending

You're the ugly sisters, to my Cinderella
You withdrew all shelter when I needed an umbrella
You're the big bad wolf, hiding in the woods
Or hunting down the little pigs, the enemy of good
You're the beastly Minotaur, lurking in the maze
You're the troll under the bridge, waiting for your prey
You're the wicked witches, of the east and west
You're the pirate Bluebeard, with his treasure chest
You're the icy snowqueen filled with poisoned rage
You're the fiendish woman who locks children in a cage
You're the dragon in the cave with fiercesome breath of fire
Did Cruella teach you how to be a nasty little liar?
You're the crone that keeps Rapunzel under lock and key
You're the dreadful Giant, the fi fo fum and fee.

But I found a pail of water and killed the wicked witch
I made it to the Prince's ball and found the shoe that fits
I followed all the bread crumbs, that clever Hansel laid
I followed Ariadne's thread, and came out of the maze
I let my long hair tumble down, from the lofty tower
I slew the dragon with my sword and found my hidden power
I chopped the mighty beanstalk down, fled to my house of brick
The wolf in bed in Granny's house did not pull off his trick
I went beyond the rainbow's end and found my pot of gold
And now my story's just begun, a new tale will be told
I found the buried treasure, the snow melted away
I crossed the bridge to pastures green
and found a brand new day.

Acknowledgements

My deepest thanks go to Julie Baker for her belief in me and for encouraging me to explore my creative side and use my words.

Thank you to Samille Mitchell for listening to my poems and encouraging me to share them.

Thank you to Phoebe Maroulis who helped me connect with the beautiful Rhianna King, and thank you, Rhianna, for your creative vision and inspiration.

To Julie Hosking, thank you for listening and helping me to "own it".

To all my friends both near and far, thank you for always being there and for your support and love across the years.

To Pam and Richard, for being a willing and appreciative audience.

To my husband and my boys, thank you for your unconditional love and for lighting up my life each day.

www.ingramcontent.com/pod-product-compliance
Lightning Source LLC
Chambersburg PA
CBHW052031290426
44112CB00014B/2461